DR. PEARL A. NELSON
8 ORCHARD LANE
WAYLAND, MASS. 01778

P. Nelson

A COMPLIMENTARY COPY from—

GARRARD PUBLISHING COMPANY
1607 NORTH MARKET STREET
CHAMPAIGN, ILLINOIS

JUNIOR SCIENCE BOOKS
Reading Level: Grade 3
Interest Level: Grades 2–5

List $2.50; Net $1.87

Junior Science Books are dedicated to all children who are eager to know more about nature and the world they live in. Written especially for young readers, each Junior Science Book has been tested by the Spache Readability Formula. The purpose of this evaluation is to assure that each book can be read by primary grade children and enjoyed by young readers through the elementary grades.

Junior Science Books are edited and designed by Nancy Larrick, Ed.D.

Junior Science Book of

Seashells

By Sam and Beryl Epstein

Illustrated by William M. Hutchinson

GARRARD PUBLISHING COMPANY
CHAMPAIGN, ILLINOIS

For assistance in checking the scientific accuracy of the text of this book, the authors and editor are grateful to Dr. Evelyn Shaw, Department of Animal Behavior, The American Museum of Natural History, New York City.

Copyright 1963 by Sam and Beryl Epstein

All rights reserved under International and Pan-American Copyright Conventions. Published in Champaign, Illinois by the Garrard Publishing Company.

Manufactured in the United States of America

Library of Congress Catalog Card Number: 62-7777

Contents

Collecting Shells	5
The Story of a Knobbed Whelk	12
The Spiral-Shaped Shells	19
Shells That Open and Close	27
Three Other Classes of Shells	39
Shell Money	44
Shells That Make Pearls	50
The Good Shell Collector	55
Index	62

Collecting Shells

There is a small sandy beach near our house. There are pebbles on it. Among the pebbles are a few shells. They seem to be the only shells on the beach.

But there are really hundreds of shells in this one small place. We can find them if we know how to look.

We wait until the tide is low. We put on boots or sneakers. We take a basket with us, and gloves. We take a shovel and a pocket knife to the beach too.

First we walk slowly along the edge of the water. We pick up a clump of wet green seaweed. We explore it with our fingers. Hidden inside we find several tiny shells. Carefully we pull them off. They are the first shells to go into our basket.

We pick up a small dark object. It looks like a slimy stone. We rub off some of the slime and discover it is really a shell.

We turn over a rock lying at the water's edge. Several small shells are clinging to the bottom. We pry them off with the knife.

A tiny jet of water squirts out of the sand. We dig at that spot with the shovel. About a foot below the surface we find a Clam.

Now we wade a little way into the water. We put on our gloves and feel among the roots of some green reeds. We find sharp-shelled Mussels among them.

We sift sand through a sieve. We find tiny shells no bigger than grains of rice.

Slowly the tide gets higher. Water covers the best hunting ground for shells. We give up our search until the next low tide.

Sometimes we go shell-hunting at night too. Then we look for shells that hide during the day. They hide in narrow cracks in the rocks. These shells come out only after dark.

On a night shell hunt we use a flashlight and move quietly. If we are quick enough, we can find many shells before they can hide again.

The first few hours after a big storm is always a good time for a shell hunt. Sometimes we find shells that we have never seen before. We know that some of them usually live deep in the water. Probably others spent their lives far to the north of us, or far to the south.

A storm brings these strange shells to Long Island, where we live. It carries them a long way through the Atlantic Ocean and into our quiet bay. Then the water tosses them on our beach. Without the storm, they might never come our way.

A good shell collector must know where to look. He must not expect to find many brightly colored shells high up on the beach.

The few shells he finds there have usually been washed ashore long before. Perhaps a storm or a very high tide brought them. Usually they are broken and faded.

People who live near the ocean can collect shells every time they go to the beach. But a beach is not the only place to find shells.

There are shells in fresh-water lakes and streams too.

And there are shells on land. You can find Snail Shells on a tree or in a garden.

Some shells are buried in the earth. Most of these are thousands of years old. They come from prehistoric times. Long

ago they were in the sea. Then the sea moved back. Shells were left on the dry land. These shells have become as hard as rock. They are called fossil shells.

There were shells on earth long before there were people. In fact, shells have existed for many millions of years.

Some ancient shells are different from any shells that live today. We know about them because we can study fossil shells.

Altogether there are about 100,000 different kinds of shells in the world. No one could ever collect them all.

But just one shell is enough to start a collection. Maybe you will find the shell yourself, and take it home and clean it. Maybe somebody will give you your first shell. Or you might buy it. Many stores sell shells.

Certainly you will want to know the name of your shell and where it came from. You will also want to know which of the five big shell classes, or groups, it belongs to. And you will want to know something about its life story.

There is a story behind every shell. Learning those stories is part of the fun of collecting shells.

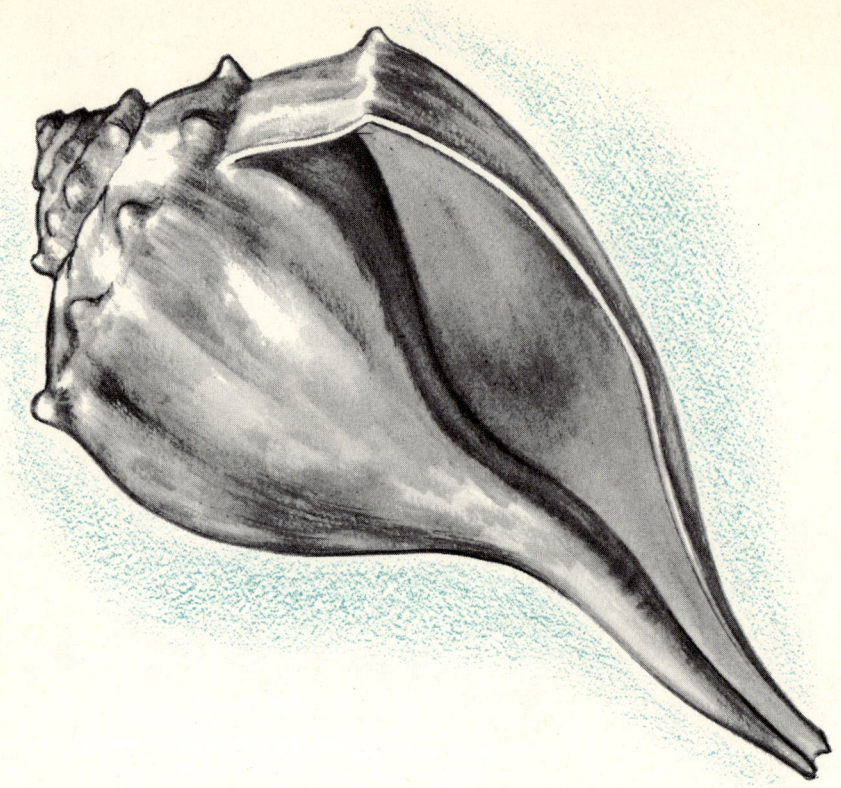

The Story of a Knobbed Whelk

The biggest shell we have found on our beach is a Knobbed Whelk. It is about nine inches long. It has a spiral shape with a point at one end. The point is called its spire. The shell is a dull yellow-gray on the outside. On the inside it is a lovely orange-red color.

The Knobbed Whelk is a common shell. It can be found all along the Atlantic coast from Cape Cod to northern Florida.

Our Knobbed Whelk is now an empty dead shell. When we found it, it was still alive. This means that the animal that made the shell was still living inside it. We had to boil the shell to remove the animal. Then we could put the Knobbed Whelk in our collection.

An animal that makes a shell is called a *mollusk*. The word means *soft body*. It describes this kind of animal very well.

The shell a mollusk makes is the only hard part of its body. Some people call the shell its home. Others say the shell is its skeleton. The shell is really both. It is the home of the mollusk and its skeleton too.

The mollusk that built our Knobbed Whelk looked like a soft grayish blob of jelly. At one end of the blob were two eyes and a mouth with a rough tongue. At the same end were two little feelers that looked like a pair of small horns.

The rest of the soft body was the mollusk's stomach and foot, all in one. Scientists call this mollusk a *Gastropod* (pronounced GAS-*troh-pod*). The name means *stomach-foot*.

On the end of a Gastropod's foot there is usually a hard layer. It is somewhat like a toenail. This hard layer is called an *Operculum* (pronounced O-PURR-*kew-lum*). This name means *lid*.

Imagine a Gastropod inside his shell. That lid closes the shell opening like a tight little door. When the Gastropod pushes his body out of his shell, the lid comes first. Then he moves along on the end of his stomach-foot.

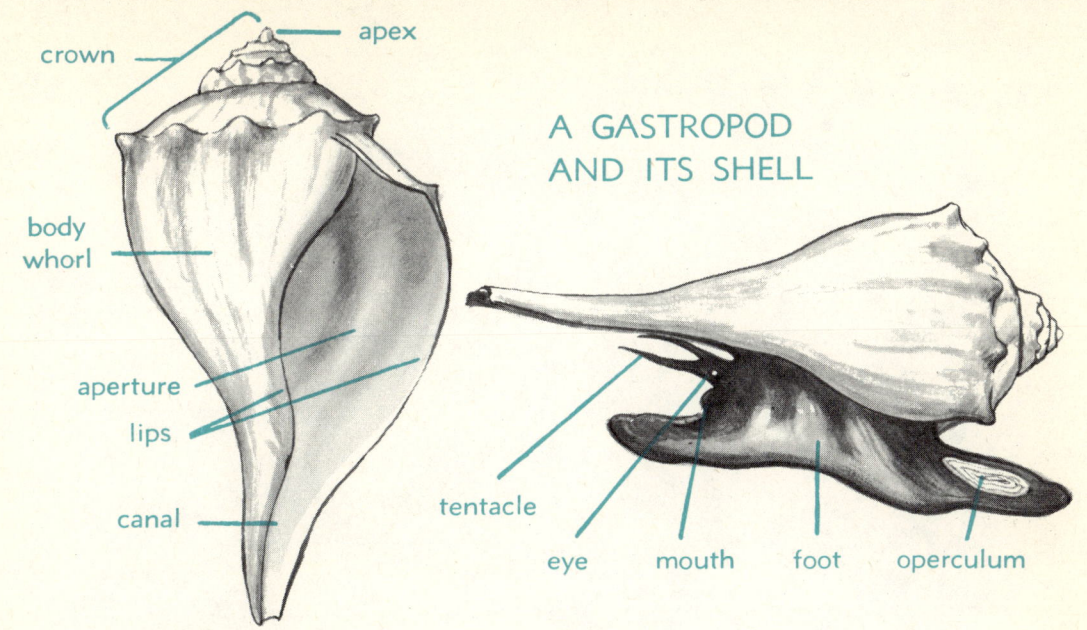

A GASTROPOD AND ITS SHELL

Our big Knobbed Whelk started life as a tiny egg. The mother Whelk laid the egg, along with several others. All were inside a little flat case. It looked like a round paper sack about the size of a nickel. The mother Whelk made the case before she laid the eggs.

She made several dozen other cases too. One came after the other. She also made the tough string or cord that held them together. The first case was fastened to a stone in shallow water at the edge of the

LIFE CYCLE OF WHELK

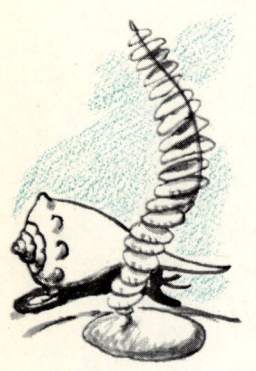 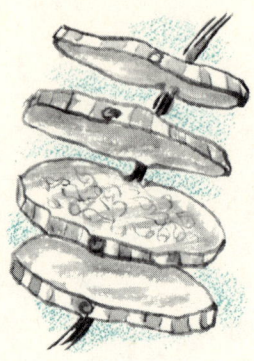 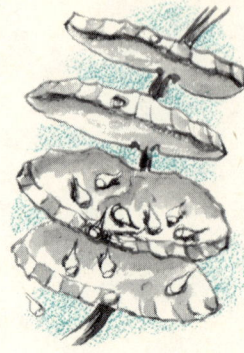 

1. Adult Whelk lays string of egg cases.
2. Eggs in each case hatch young Whelks.
3. At proper time tiny young Whelks emerge.
4. Each small Whelk begins life alone.

   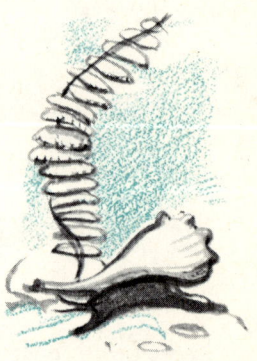

5. Small Whelk moves about and grows.
6. Growing Whelk finds food on sea floor.
7. Infant Whelk grows larger and matures.
8. Mature Whelk lays string of egg cases.

sea. The egg cases floated up from the stone. They looked like a string of flat yellowish-white beads.

Soon the eggs hatched inside the egg cases. Each one became a tiny Gastropod. Each was inside a tiny Whelk shell about a quarter of an inch long. Then the cases broke open, and the baby Whelks began their own lives.

Each Gastropod started to grow. As it grew, it added to its shell.

Shell-building is done by the thin outer layer of a mollusk's soft body. This layer is called a *mantle*. The mantle gives off a substance that quickly turns hard. It becomes new shell.

The shell of our Knobbed Whelk grew larger and larger.

Of course the Gastropod inside the shell needed food in order to grow. So it pushed its stomach-foot outside its shell and moved about. Its tongue scraped up small dead sea animals from the sand. The rough surface of the tongue tore the food into tiny bits.

A Knobbed Whelk often eats Clams. It may do this by drilling a hole in a Clam shell. Or it may open a Clam's hard shell. To do this it folds its stomach-foot around a Clam. Then it pushes the hard lip of its own shell between the two shells of the Clam. At the same time, the Whelk's strong stomach-foot sucks at the Clam shells, to pull them open. Finally the Whelk's rough tongue gets inside the Clam shell. Then the Gastropod can eat the soft Clam.

The Spiral-Shaped Shells

There are many kinds of Whelks. All belong to one big class, or group. These are the spiral-shaped shells, often called the Snails.

All Snails belong to this class. So do many other kinds of shells.

Some are no bigger than a pinhead. Others are more than two feet long and weigh several pounds. Some are rough on the outside. These may be covered with knobs or bumps or sharp spines. Others are smooth and shiny. Some are dull gray or white. Others are brightly colored.

Many of these shells have names that tell us what they look like.

A Cone Shell may be shaped like a cone. Some of them have beautiful markings.

The marks on one kind of Cone Shell look like letters of the alphabet. It is called the Alphabet Cone. An Alphabet Cone is only two or three inches long. But it is the biggest Cone Shell on the Atlantic coast.

Another Cone Shell is called the Glory-of-the-Sea. It is very rare and valuable. It is found in the East Indies and the Philippines. One Glory-of-the-Sea Cone is worth hundreds of dollars.

A Turret Shell looks like the tip of a

turret, or tower. It is found on both the Atlantic and Pacific coasts.

Top Shells, with spiral markings, look like spinning tops. They, too, are found on both coasts of the United States.

The round white Moon Shell is found along the north Atlantic coast. It looks like a small shiny moon.

When a Moon Shell mollusk is ready to lay its eggs, it cements grains of sand together. They form a sort of flat round collar. The mollusk lays its eggs among the grains of sand in this odd sand collar.

Moon Shell and Sand Collars

The Trumpet Shell does not look like a modern trumpet. But in ancient times it was used as a trumpet. First someone cut a hole in the pointed tip of the shell. Then he blew through that hole. The sound was low and sad, rather like a foghorn.

Perhaps you have seen a picture of Triton, the ancient Greek god of the sea. He is usually shown blowing into one of these shells. Sometimes they are called Triton Shells.

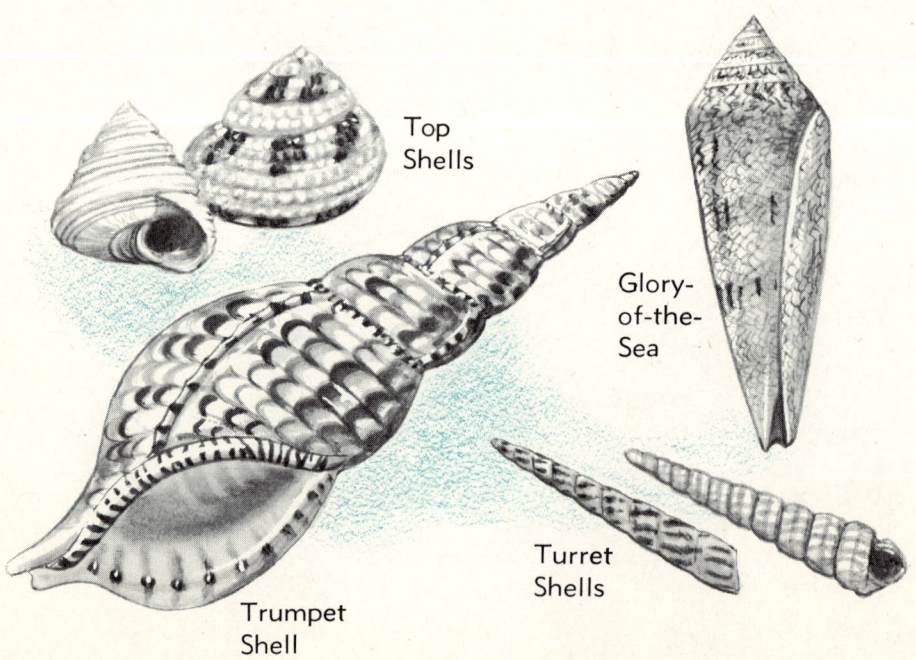

Top Shells

Glory-of-the-Sea

Turret Shells

Trumpet Shell

Abalone

Limpets and Abalone Shells do not look much like the other members of this class. They start out as spiral-shaped shells. But as they grow, they become flat. They come to look like saucers or shallow bowls.

Limpets are usually quite small. Some of them cling to rocks most of the time, or to seaweed. One kind has a hole in the middle that looks like a keyhole. It is called the Keyhole Limpet.

An Abalone Shell is sometimes as big as a large soup bowl, or even bigger. It lives clamped up tightly against a rock. The mollusk inside sucks in water through a row of small holes. They are in the edge of his shell. Water gives the animal the food and oxygen it needs.

The outside of an Abalone Shell is dull and rough. The smooth inside is colored in lovely shades of green, blue, red and pink. Most Abalones are found on the Pacific coast. Only one kind lives on the Atlantic coast, and it is very rare.

The Abalone mollusk is quite tough, but many people think it is good to eat. They pound it to make it tender. Then they cut it up into Abalone steaks.

Many mollusks from spiral-shaped shells are used for food. For example, Snails are popular in Europe. And the big mollusk

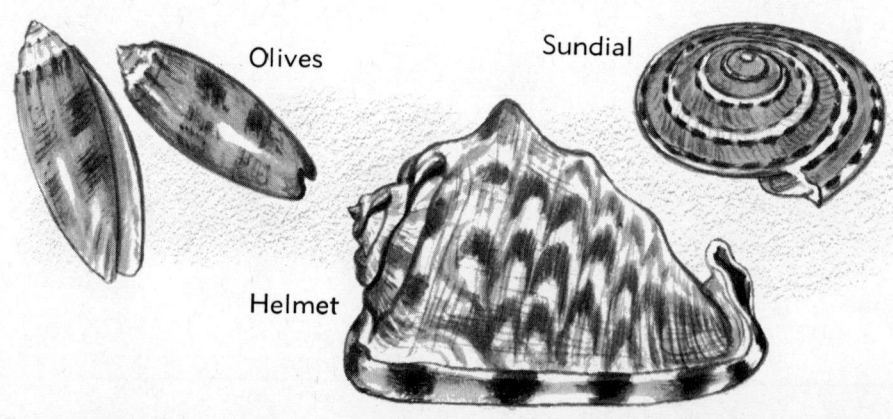

Olives

Sundial

Helmet

inside a curling Conch Shell is popular in Europe and the West Indies.

The Conch (pronounced *konk*) looks something like a Whelk. The Conch is the shell that seems to make a roaring sound. Hold it against your ear. You hear a sound like the roaring of the sea. It is really air inside the shell which vibrates against your eardrum.

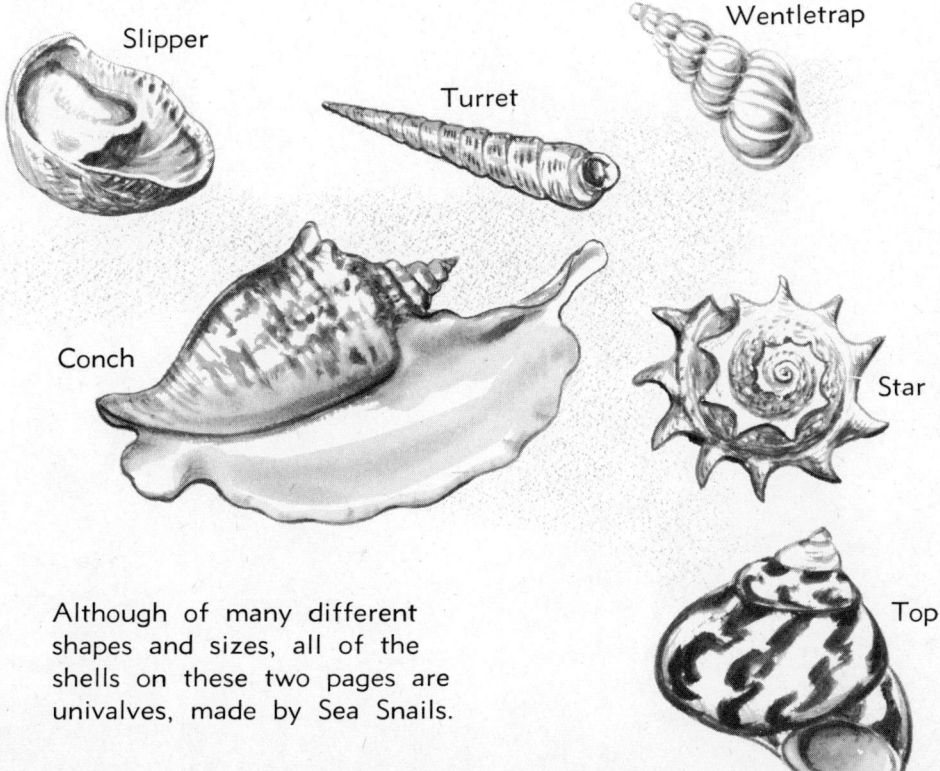

Although of many different shapes and sizes, all of the shells on these two pages are univalves, made by Sea Snails.

Another spiral-shaped shell is sharp and spiny. It is called a Murex. When the shell is crushed, it gives a deep purplish-red liquid. Hundreds of years ago men used the Murex to make dye.

Every spiral-shaped shell is made by a Gastropod, or stomach-foot mollusk. A Gastropod always makes his shell in one piece. Scientists call this a valve. This kind of shell is known as a *univalve*. (*Uni* means one.)

The univalves form the biggest of the five big classes of shells.

Shells That Open and Close

Some shells have two parts, or valves. These are called *bivalves*. (*Bi* means *two*.) The bivalves are the second largest of the five big classes of shells.

The two parts of a bivalve are hinged together. They can open and close like the covers of a book.

The biggest mollusk in the world is a bivalve. It is called the Giant Clam. It may be three or even four feet wide. Both parts of its shell have deep curves along their edges. When the shell is closed, the curves fit snugly together.

The lining of the Giant Clam is smooth and white. It seems like white china. Half of this big shell would make a good bathtub for a baby. Even a small child could use it. Years ago, in the South Sea Islands, people baptized their children in Giant Clam Shells.

Deep-sea divers are afraid of this big Clam. If the shell should close on a diver's hand, he would be caught. No wonder this big mollusk is sometimes called the Man-Eating Clam! It is also called the Man Trap.

All Clams belong to this same class. One

of the smallest is the Gem Clam. It is not much bigger than the period at the end of this sentence.

Oysters are bivalves too. One of the strangest is the Tree Oyster. It clings to the roots of trees in Florida swamps. Other strange Oysters, called Thorny Oysters, are covered with sharp spines, or thorns.

Some bivalves spend their lives in one place. Oysters drift for a few days or a week when they are first born. Then they stick to some hard surface and never move. Sometimes hundreds of oysters settle down close together on the sea bottom. They form what is known as an Oyster bed.

An Oyster fisherman often "plants" young Oysters near the coast. He leaves them to grow up there. Then he can gather the oysters very easily when they are big enough to sell. Many of these planted Oyster beds are off the coast of Maryland and New Jersey. Both states are famous for fine Oysters. On the New Jersey coast there is a town called Bivalve. Most of the people in that town earn their living by gathering Oysters and selling them.

Mollusks that never move are in great danger from their enemies. The Oyster has two dangerous enemies. One is a small Snail called the Oyster Drill. The other is the Starfish.

A tiny Oyster Drill can drill a hole through an Oyster shell. Then it sucks out the Oyster's soft body and eats it.

A Starfish clamps its pointed arms

around an Oyster. It pulls the Oyster shell open and eats the soft body inside.

Not all bivalves spend their lives in one spot. Some move once in a while. Some move more often.

A Mussel spins threads, like the threads of a spider's web. It uses these threads to fasten itself to a rock or some other hard surface. Sometimes a Mussel spins new threads and fastens them to a new spot. Then it leaves the old threads and pulls itself to a new home.

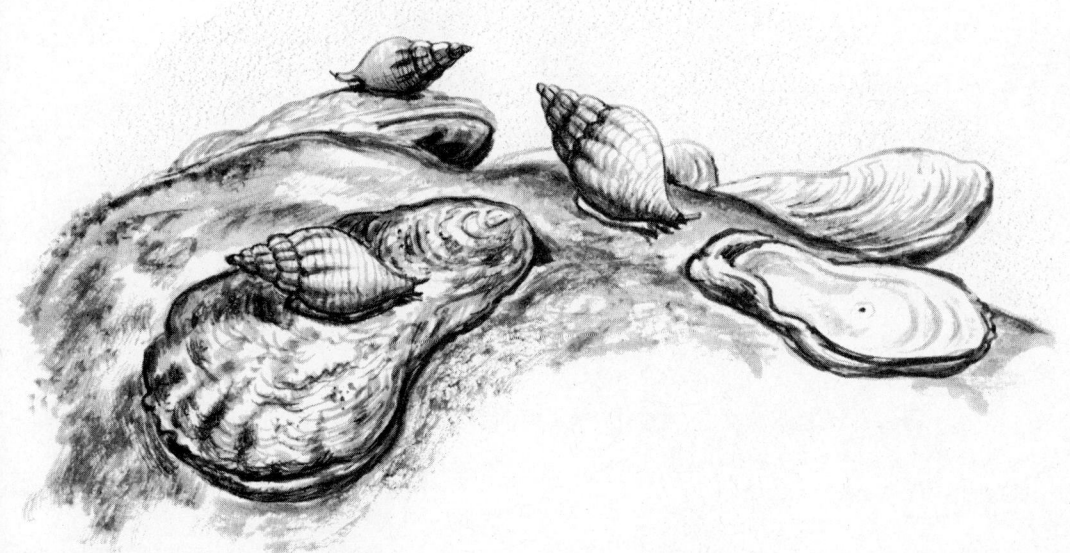

Scallop takes water in through front.

Scallop forces water out hinged end, moving forward.

A Clam can dig itself deep into the sand. There it is usually safe from its enemies.

A Scallop can bounce along the sea bottom. It moves by jet propulsion like a rocket.

The Scallop opens the two parts of its shell and takes in water. Then it closes the shell quickly. As the shell snaps shut, the water is pushed out through the hinge end. This jet of water squirts backward. This sends the Scallop forward in a kind of jump.

Scallops look funny, bouncing along under

the water. But their scalloped, fan-shaped shells are very pretty. Some are grayish or brownish. Others are pink or yellow or red. Some are striped. Some are spotted.

Many artists have copied the Scallop's lovely shape. Perhaps you have seen a stone fountain carved in the shape of a Scallop Shell. Perhaps you have seen a Scallop Shell carved in wood over a doorway. Or you may have seen a picture of Saint James holding a Scallop Shell. This shell is his special symbol, because he was a fisherman.

Long ago, when people visited a shrine of Saint James, they brought back Scallop Shells as souvenirs. The Scallop Shells proved they had been on a long trip. Sometimes a knight put a Scallop Shell on his shield. It showed he had been on a long journey.

Today you can see a big Scallop Shell over certain filling stations. These are the gasoline stations of the Shell Oil Company. Not many people know that the Scallop Shell is an ancient symbol for a journey.

The mollusk that builds a bivalve is called a *Pelecypoda* (pronounced *pel-e-*SIP*-oh-dah*). Its soft body has a foot that pushes into the sand. Sometimes the foot

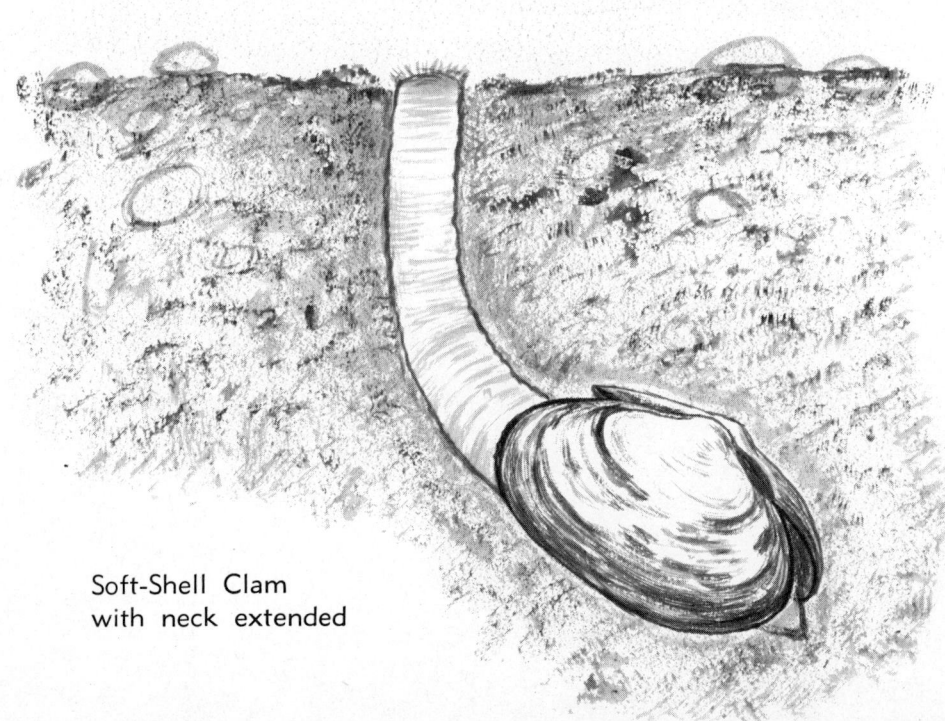

Soft-Shell Clam
with neck extended

is shaped like a hatchet. Pelecypoda means *hatchet-foot*.

This bivalve mollusk has a different body from the mollusk of a univalve. The Scallop has a row of eyes around its body. But most bivalves have no eyes at all—and no mouths either. Clams, for example, take food and oxygen out of the water through tubes called *necks*. When a Clam buries itself in the sand, it pokes a neck up into the water. It is hidden from its enemies. But it can still eat and breathe.

A Hard-Shell Clam has a short neck. That is why it never buries itself very deep. Big Hard-Shell Clams are called Quahogs. Smaller ones are called Cherrystones. The littlest ones are called Little Neck Clams.

The neck of the Soft-Shell Clam is much longer. It can stretch out longer than the Clam's shell. That is why the Soft-

Shell Clam can bury itself deep in the sand. Another name for this Clam is Long Neck. Still another name is Steamer. That is because people often cook this Clam in hot steam.

Bivalves have strong muscles which open and close their shells. The Scallop's muscle, for example, is firm and white. The rest of its body is gray and very soft. When you eat a Scallop, you are really eating only the mollusk's white hinge muscle.

One bivalve is a serious enemy to mankind. It looks like a white worm about the size of a pencil. For many years people thought it really was a worm. Then they discovered a pair of tiny shells at one end of its body. These shells prove it is in the Clam group. It is called a Shipworm.

A Shipworm can use its shells to bore holes in wood. In five weeks it can bore a

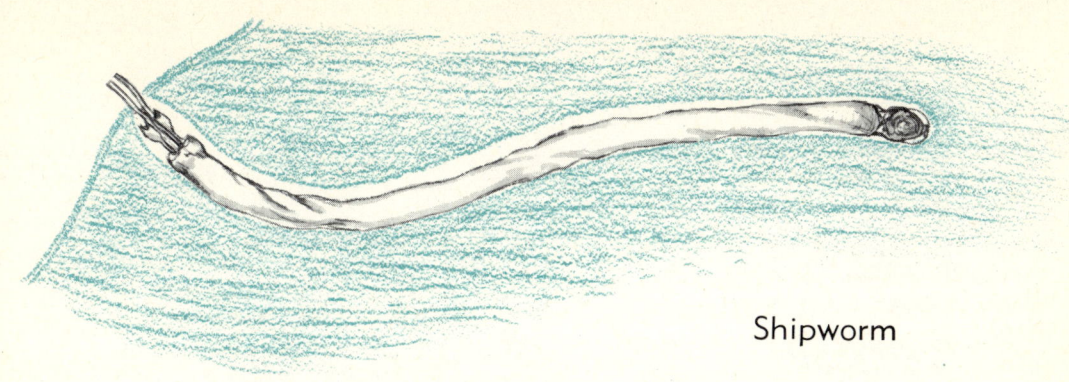

Shipworm

hole four inches long through the hardest wood. Hundreds of Shipworms will bore at the wooden pilings of a wharf. In just a few months, they can eat it away. Shipworms can destroy wooden ships too.

Once they almost caused a flood in Holland. They bored into the wooden

Wood bored by Shipworms

timbers that supported the dikes. The timbers began to collapse. Experts found the damage just in time. The dikes were saved, and a great flood was prevented.

As a whole the bivalves are probably more useful to human beings than any other shell animals.

All over the world people eat bivalve mollusks—Clams, Oysters, Scallops and Mussels. Bivalve shells are also useful in many ways. Buttons are made out of smooth shell linings. Small bivalves are made into jewelry. They are used to decorate boxes and picture frames and many other things.

And every year thousands of tons of Clam shells and Oyster shells are ground into powder. It is sold as fertilizer. This fertilizer helps to improve crops because shells contain the lime most plants need.

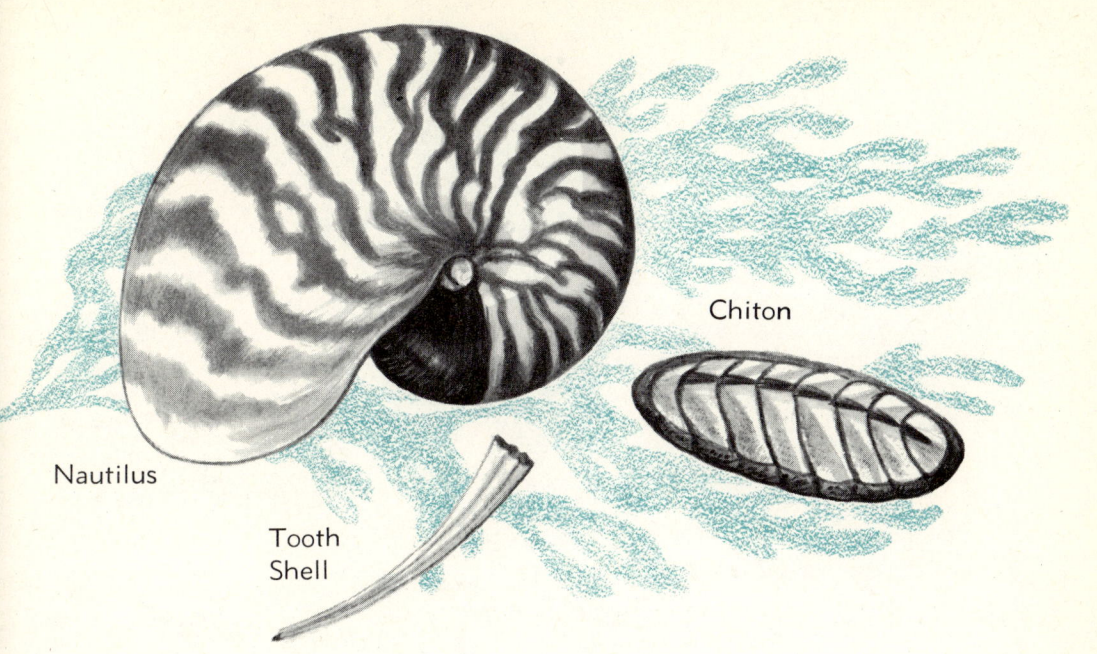

Three Other Classes of Shells

Most of the shells that people collect are either univalves or bivalves. There are three smaller classes of shells that are very interesting too. These are the Chitons (pronounced KITE-*ons*), the Tooth Shells and the Nautilus Shells.

A Chiton has eight separate shells, or plates. These are held together by a tough

39

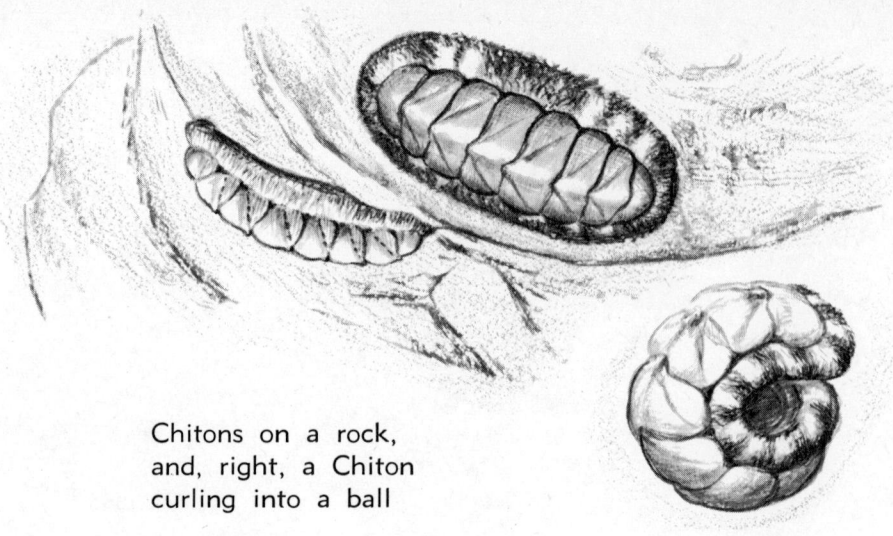

Chitons on a rock, and, right, a Chiton curling into a ball

leathery band. The shells overlap. They remind you of the metal plates of a coat of mail worn by a knight in armor. A Chiton is sometimes called a Coat-of-Mail Shell. Scientists call it an *Amphineura* (pronounced *am-fi-*NOO*-rah*).

Most Chitons are only an inch or two long. But the Giant Pacific Chiton grows as much as a foot long.

Chitons live mostly along the Pacific coast. They fasten themselves to the undersides of rocks. With a knife you can pry a Chiton from a rock. Then it will curl up into a ball. If you drop it in sea water right away, it will uncurl again.

A Tooth Shell is a one-piece shell, usually about an inch long. It is really a small curved hollow tube, open at both ends. Usually it is white. It looks like an animal tooth or a tiny animal tusk. Sometimes it is called a Tusk Shell. Its scientific name is *Scaphopoda* (pronounced *ska-*FOP*-o-dah*). It too is found along the Pacific coast.

A Nautilus Shell looks like some of the spiral-shaped shells. Its scientific name is *Cephalopoda* (pronounced *sef-a-*LOP*-o-dah*). But the mollusk inside a Nautilus Shell is not a Gastropod. It is related to the Squid and the Cuttlefish. Indeed it looks a good deal like those curious sea animals.

The mouth of the Nautilus Shell mollusk is surrounded by almost a hundred tiny arms. These are called *tentacles*. Those

Nautilus Shell

tentacles make up its foot. They snatch food out of the water and push it into the mollusk's mouth.

The Nautilus starts life in a single tiny shell room, or chamber. When it grows larger, it builds a second room next to the first one. Then it moves into the new room and seals off the old one. After a time it makes a third room, and then a fourth, and so on. The rooms follow one another in a spiral. Each room is larger than the one before it. The Nautilus mollusk always lives inside its newest and largest room.

This mollusk's relatives, the Squid and the Cuttlefish, also make shells. But their shells are inside their bodies, not on the outside. The shells are thin and flat. They are shaped like a slender leaf, or a feather.

The bone, or shell, inside a Cuttlefish is called a cuttlebone. People often put a piece of cuttlebone in a bird cage. The lime in the shell is good for birds. And birds seem to enjoy pecking away at the hard white shell.

Cuttlefish

Squid

Shell Money

Many different kinds of shells have been used as money.

American Indians on the Pacific coast used Tooth Shells as money. Sometimes they carried them in a purse of elk horn.

Sometimes they strung them on thin strips of animal skin and wore them around their necks. A rich man could show off his wealth by wearing many strings of Tooth Shells.

Some shells were worth more than others. The ones that were most difficult to find were worth the most. One rare Tooth Shell might be worth as much as a five-dollar bill today.

Indians living along the Atlantic coast did not use whole shells as money. Instead they made beads from the shells of Clams and Whelks. They called these wampum.

A piece of wampum was made from the smooth lining of a shell. The bead might be round and flat, like a coin. Or it might be oval. Sometimes it was long and thin like a piece of drinking straw.

The most valuable wampum was made

from the narrow dark border inside a Clam shell. It was called black wampum. White wampum was made from Whelk shells. It was not worth as much as black wampum.

English settlers who came to America tried to make wampum. They wanted to use it for buying things from the Indians. But it took a long time to carve a shell bead by hand and then drill a hole through it. They said, "Only Indians have the time and patience to make wampum."

Then new tools were invented. Soon the settlers were making thousands of shell beads. Wampum became very common. A shell bead was worth no more than a broken shell, or a handful of sand.

Finally the Indians, and the white people too, stopped using wampum as money. It had become worthless. They used metal coins instead. But many Indians still wore shell bead necklaces and belts. They sewed shell beads on their clothes.

Cowrie Shells have been used as money too, especially in Asia, Africa and the South Sea Islands. Cowries are shiny spiral-shaped shells. They are found mostly in the warm waters of the Pacific and in the Indian Ocean.

Cowrie money was so popular that it spread all over the world. It even got to America. It must have reached America after a long journey through many lands.

Perhaps an African trader bought some silk in China. He paid for it with Cowrie Shells. Then the Chinese silk merchant may have used those shells to buy seal skins.

These skins came from Russian fur trappers in Alaska. The Russian trappers may have used the same shells to buy meat or fish from Indians on the Pacific coast. And those Indians may have traded the shells to other Indians. Finally the Cowrie Shells from Africa reached the hands of Indians living in Massachusetts or Connecticut.

Less than 50 years ago, Cowrie Shells were still being used as money in a few parts of the world.

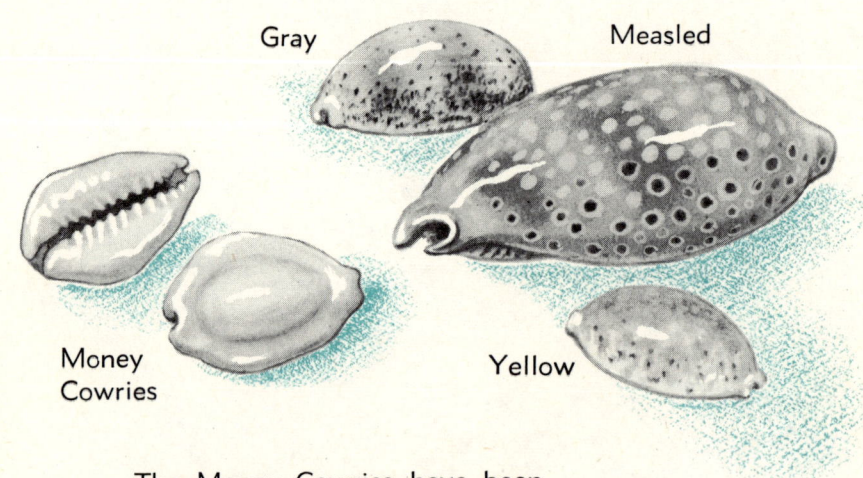

The Money Cowries have been used as money in many parts of the world. Shown with them are three North American Cowries.

Cowrie Shells from Africa passed in trade along the route shown below from Old China to American Indians in what is now New England.

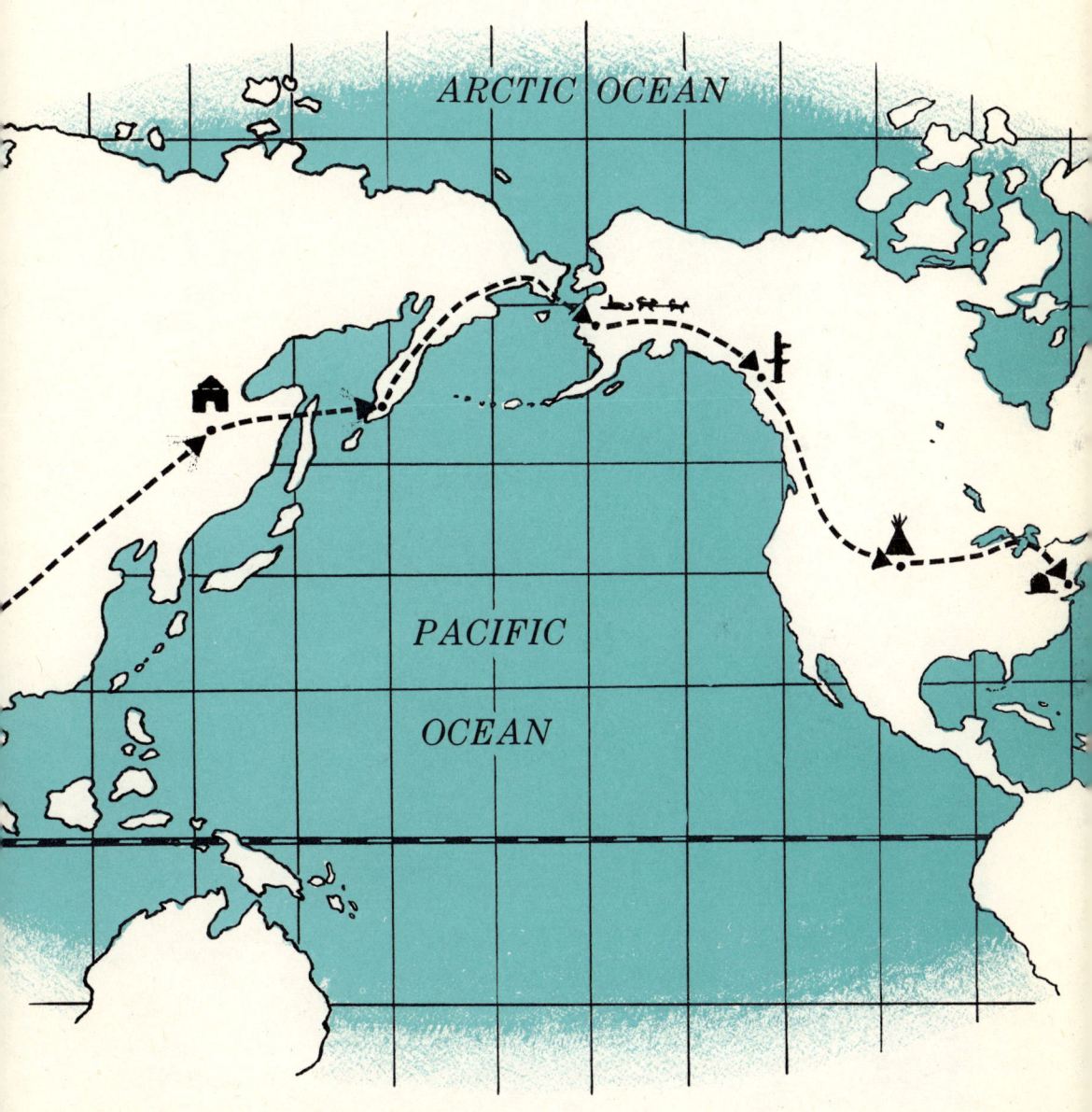

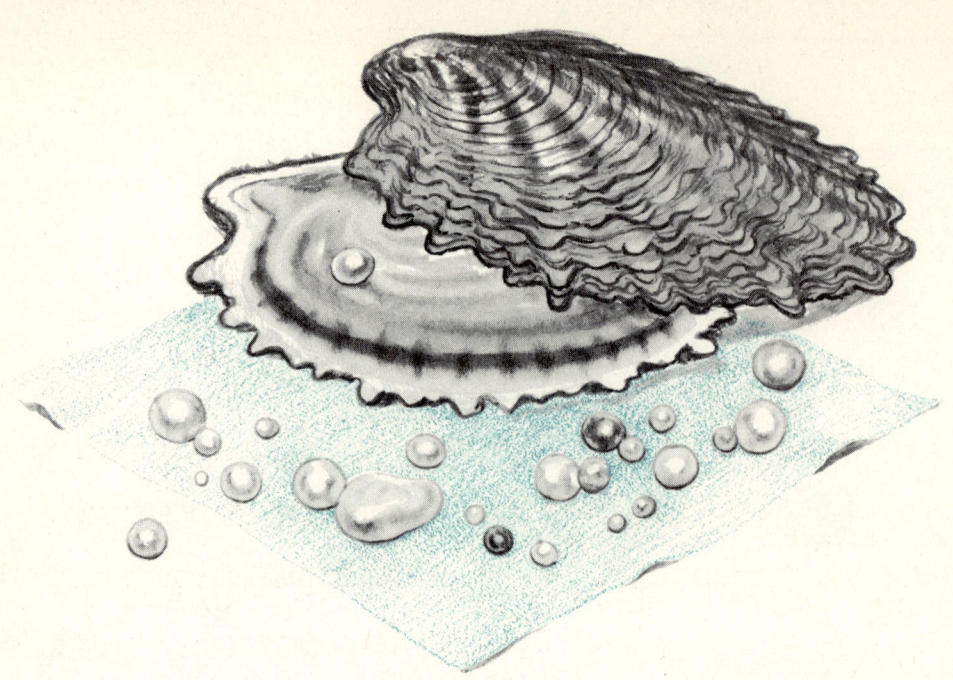

Shells That Make Pearls

People who eat Oysters sometimes say, "Perhaps I will find a pearl." They almost never do. And when they do, the pearl is usually small and dull. It is not worth very much.

The Oysters in which pearls are found are not the kind that people usually eat. They are a special kind called Pearl

Oysters. They live only in the warm waters of the Pacific and Indian Oceans.

The shells of Pearl Oysters are rough on the outside. But their inside lining is smooth and shiny. In the light, it shows a faint glow of many colors. This lining is what we call mother-of-pearl. Often buttons are made out of it. The scientific name used for mother-of-pearl is *nacre* (pronounced NAY-*ker*).

A pearl begins as a grain of sand or some other tiny object.

Sometimes this grain of sand gets into an Oyster. It is rough against the Oyster's soft body. So the Oyster coats the sand with nacre. This is the same smooth stuff that lines its shell. A few layers of nacre make only a small pearl. As more layers are added, the pearl grows larger.

Divers who search for Pearl Oysters have

a hard and dangerous job. Usually they bring up hundreds of shells before they find one good pearl. That is why a good real pearl is so rare and expensive. This kind of pearl is called a *natural pearl*.

It is possible to "fool" an Oyster into making a pearl. A hole is drilled in an Oyster shell. A tiny bead of nacre is put into the Oyster's body. Only an expert can do this without killing the Oyster. But if the Oyster lives, it may cover the bead with more nacre. This is the beginning of a pearl. This kind of pearl is called a *cultured pearl*.

Pearl Oysters are not the only shells that make pearls. Sometimes other kinds of shells do too. In each case, the shell makes a pearl that looks like the shell's own lining.

The Giant Clam can make a giant pearl

as big as a baby's fist. It looks like a lump of white china. That is because the Giant Clam's lining looks like white china.

Sometimes an Abalone makes a pearl. An Abalone pearl is as bright as the shell's lining. It may be green or blue or yellow.

The big spiral-shaped Queen Conch has a lovely pink lining. It can produce a beautiful pink pearl.

Fresh-water Mussels also produce fine pearls. Indians used to gather these pearls and wear them. Many Mussel pearls have been found in Indian graves.

One time the Empress of France paid $25,000 for a beautiful Mussel pearl. It had been found in New Jersey. This Queen Pearl, as it was called, became one of the most famous in the world.

The Good Shell Collector

A shell collector looks for shells whenever he has the chance. He may buy shells too. He may also trade shells with other collectors.

If he lives on the Pacific coast, for example, he may trade shells with someone who lives on the Atlantic coast. In this way both collectors add new shells to their collections.

A shell collector also learns how to clean his shells.

The first step is to take out the mollusk that may still be alive inside. Usually the easiest way to do this is to boil the shell in water. This kills the mollusk. Then it is fairly easy to scrape the soft mollusk out of its shell. Afterward the shell should be carefully washed and dried. A stiff brush helps to remove sand and slime.

Most collectors like to label their shells. A good label tells:

1. The name of the shell
2. The class it belongs to
3. Where it was found
4. When it was found

It is not always easy to learn the name of a shell. Perhaps a science teacher can help you. In the library you may find a book about shells.

Look at pictures of shells. Try to find a picture like the strange shell you have. Or visit a museum or shop that has a good shell collection. Try to match your strange shell to one on exhibit.

Arranging a shell collection is important, too. Some arrange their shells by class. The univalves are on one shelf. The bivalves are on another.

Other collectors arrange shells by color or by size. Perhaps you have shells from different places. You may want to keep all the shells from one place together.

You can keep your shells in boxes or in

the drawers of a chest. You may want to keep them glued to sheets of cardboard.

Shell collectors like to learn everything they can about shells. They read books about them. They look at shell collections in museums and shops. They talk to experts who can give them hints about finding and cleaning and arranging shells.

An expert may recognize a shell that is valuable because it is a freak.

Here is a Knobbed Whelk, for example. To some people it might look like all other Knobbed Whelks. But an expert knows that most Knobbed Whelks twist toward the right. This one twists toward the left. So an expert would know that this shell is valuable because it is a freak. He would call it a Left-Handed Knobbed Whelk.

The Lightning Whelk, common in Florida, usually twists toward the left. A Lightning

Whelk with a right-hand twist would be rare and valuable.

Most shell collectors hope to find a shell that no one has ever found before. Once in a while this happens. Probably there are many kinds of shells in the world that no one has yet found.

Every shell hunt is as exciting as a treasure hunt. Every shell collector is sure he will find some new and wonderful shell for his collection.

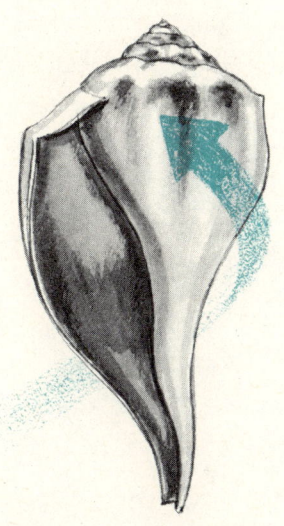 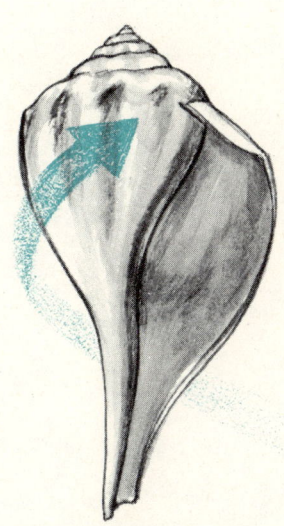

Freak Whelk twists to left.   Normal Whelk twists to right.

SOME COMMON SHELLS AND WHERE THEY ARE FOUND

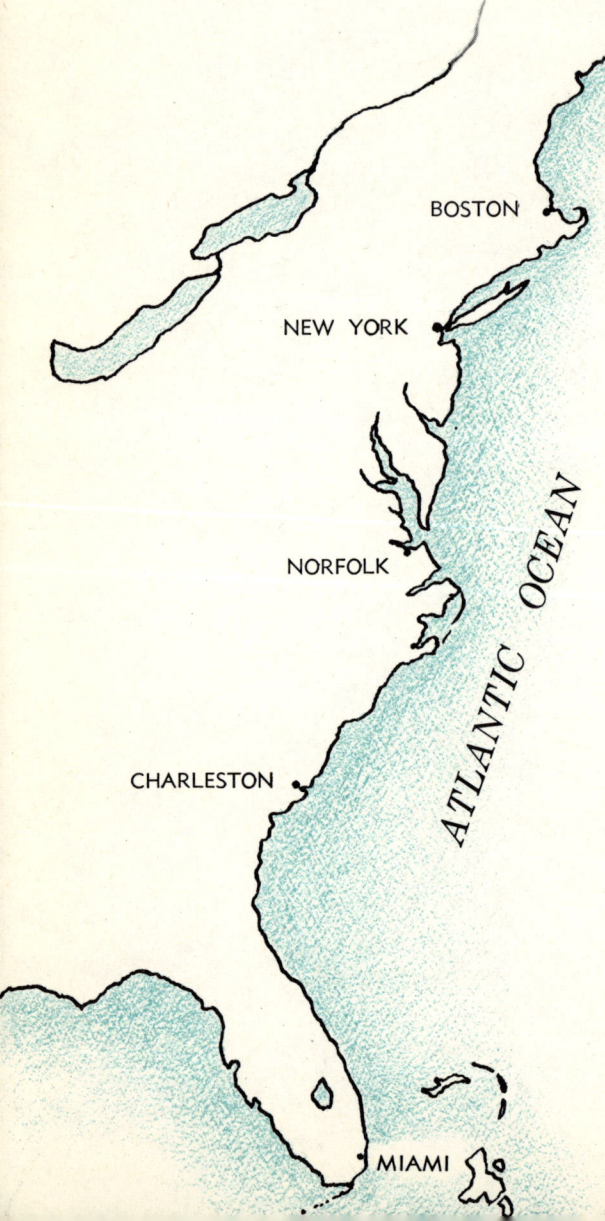

North Atlantic Coast
Whelks
Scallops
Hard-Shell Clams
Soft-Shell Clams
Jingle Shells
Cockle Shells
Moon Shells
Ark Shells
Oysters
Mussels

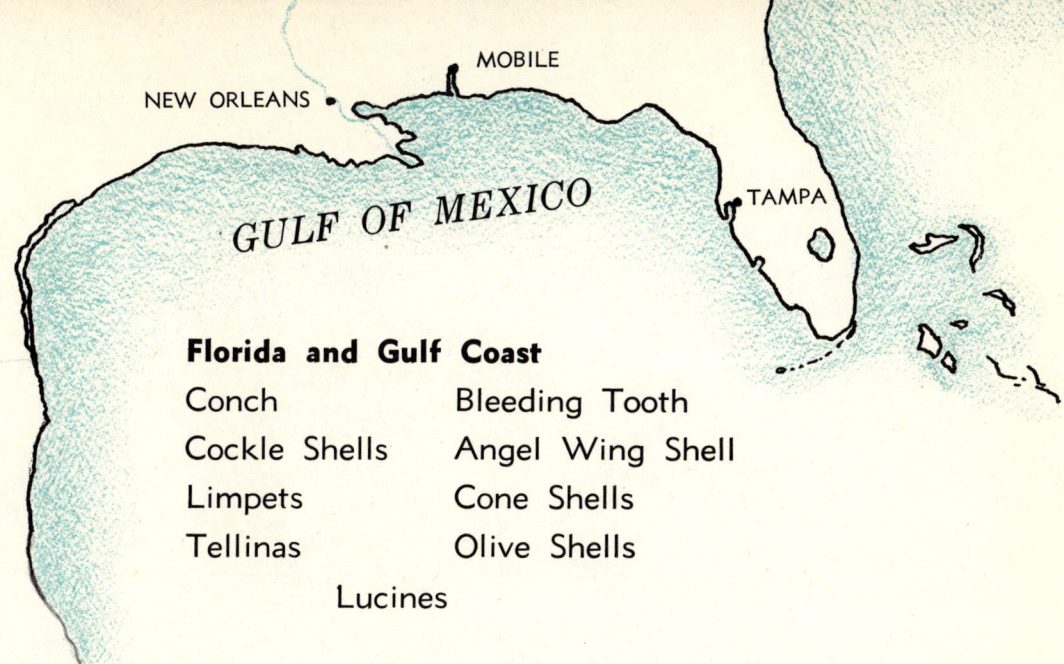

Florida and Gulf Coast

Conch
Cockle Shells
Limpets
Tellinas
Lucines
Bleeding Tooth
Angel Wing Shell
Cone Shells
Olive Shells

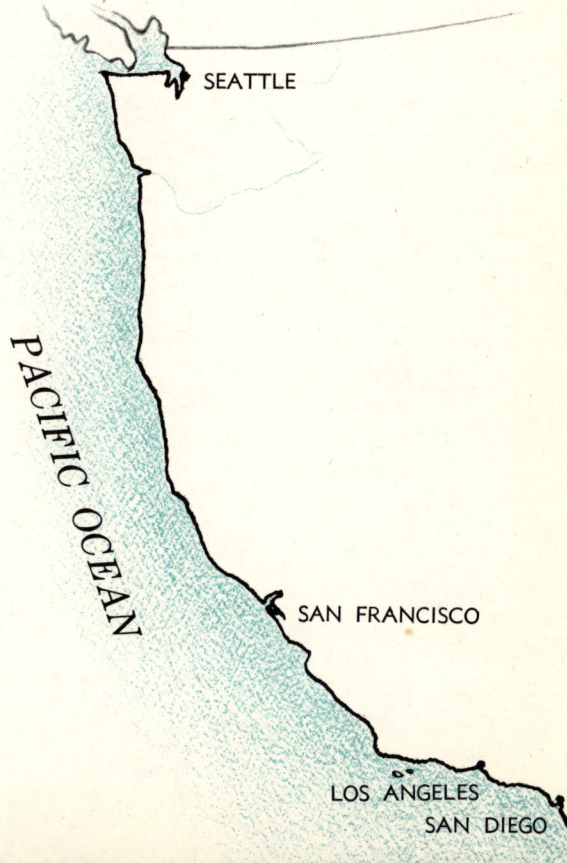

Pacific Coast

Abalones
Giant Clams
Giant Chitons
Giant Limpets
Giant Pod Shells
Tooth Shells

Index

Abalone, 23-24, 54, 61
Alphabet cone shell, 20
Amphineura, 40
Angel wing shell, 61
Ark shell, 60

Bivalves, 27-38
Bleeding tooth, 57, 61

Cephalopoda, 41
Cherrystone clam, 35
Chiton, 39-41
Clam, 6, 18, 28-29, 32, 35, 38, 45-46
Coat-of-mail shell, 40
Cockle shell, 60, 61
Cone shell, 20, 61
Conch shell, 25, 61
Cowrie shell, 47-48
Cuttlefish, 41, 43

Fossil shells, 10

Gastropod, 14, 15, 17-18, 26
Gem clam, 29
Giant chiton, 61
Giant clam, 28, 52-54, 61
Giant limpet, 61
Giant Pacific chiton, 40
Giant pod shell, 61
Glory-of-the-sea, 20, 22

Hard-shell clam, 35, 60
Helmet shell, 24

Jingle shell, 57, 60

Keyhole limpet, 23

Knobbed whelk, 12-18, 45, 60
   Birth and growth, 15-18
   Description, 12
   Food, 18
   Left-handed, 58, 59
   Location, 13

Lightning whelk, 58-59
Little neck clam, 35
Limpet, 23, 61
Lucine, 61

Mantle, 17
Mollusk
   Abalone, 23-24
   Knobbed whelk, 13-14
   Moon shell, 21
   Nautilus, 41-42
   Oyster, 30
   Removing from shell, 56
   Scallop, 36
   Use as food, 24-25, 36, 38
      See also Gastropod, Pelecypoda
Moon shell, 21, 60
Mother-of-pearl, 51
Murex, 26
Mussel, 7, 31, 38, 54, 60

Nacre, 51
Nautilus shell, 39, 41-42

Olive shell, 24, 61
Operculum, 14, 15, 18
Oyster, 29-31, 38, 50-52, 60
Oyster beds, 29-30
Oyster drill, 30

Pearl oyster, 50-52
Pearls
  Cultured, 52
  Natural, 52-54
Pelecypoda, 34-35

Quahogs, 35
Queen conch, 54

Scallop, 32-34, 35, 36, 38, 60
Scaphopoda, 41
Shell money, 44-49
Shipworm, 36-38
Slipper shell, 25
Snail, 10, 19, 24
Soft-shell clam, 34, 35-36, 60
Spiral-shaped shells, 19-26
Squid, 41, 43

Starfish, 30-31
Star shell, 25
Sundial shell, 24

Tellina, 61
Thorny oyster, 29
Tooth shell, 39, 41, 44-45, 61
Top shell, 21, 22, 25
Tree oyster, 29
Triton, 22
Trumpet shell, 22, 25
Turret shell, 20-21, 22
Tusk shell, 41

Univalves, 25, 26

Wampum, 45-47
Wentletrap, 25

ABOUT THE AUTHORS

SAM and BERYL EPSTEIN, husband and wife, have a home at the edge of Peconic Bay on Long Island. They keep a small boat tied up at their dock, dig clams on their beach, and hunt for scallops in the shallow water just offshore.

Together or separately, the Epsteins have written more than sixty books. Most of their writing for young people is in the fields of science and biography. They enjoy traveling, and make frequent trips in search of material for their books. When they were writing the *Junior Science Book of Seashells* they went shell-hunting not only along the beaches near their home, but in Florida and Mexico too.

Sam Epstein was born in Boston, Massachusetts, and Mrs. Epstein is a native of Columbus, Ohio. Both Mr. and Mrs. Epstein did editorial work before they began to devote their full time to writing books for children.

ABOUT THE ARTIST

WILLIAM M. HUTCHINSON spent the summers of his childhood at the home of an uncle in the Blue Ridge Mountains of Virginia. There he first enjoyed the study of natural history, which has remained one of his interests.

During World War II, Mr. Hutchinson served in the Pacific for three years. He collected many shell specimens in his travels from island to island and became fascinated by the variety and uses of the shells. After his return to the U. S. he learned to know the shells of the colder Atlantic waters.

A native of Norfolk, Virginia, Mr. Hutchinson attended art schools in Cleveland and New York. He works as an illustrator in the advertising and book fields and has illustrated many children's books, including several concerned with marine life.

DR. PEARL A. NELSON
8 ORCHARD LANE
WAYLAND, MASS. 01778